Grin & ferret

For my father, Floyd,
whose example has been my guide
to life, and with whom I share a
special love of ferrets.

—Jeanne

# Grin & Ferret

## A Warm and Fuzzy Guide to Life

Photographs by Jeanne Carley

**Andrews McMeel
Publishing**

Kansas City

ISBN: 0-7407-0132-0

# Grin
# & Ferret

## A Warm and Fuzzy Guide to Life

Sleep in after a good party.

Add some romance to your life.

Look at nature up close.

Get to know your neighbors.

# Experience different cultures.

Make time for naps.

Reread your favorite book.

Live life in the fast lane.

Every once in a while,
remind everyone
how cute you are.

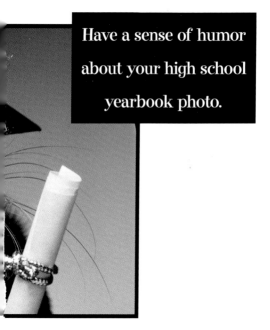

Have a sense of humor about your high school yearbook photo.

Spend quality time
with the one you love.

Drive a fun car.

# Play in the rain.

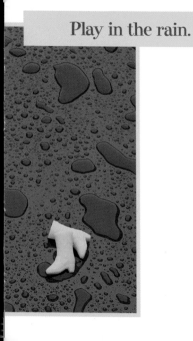

Let 'em know
what you <u>really</u> think.

When all else fails,
put on a cute hat.

Bundle up out there!

Learn about your ancestors.

When going to the beach,
bring along plenty of toys . . .

... and wear something that doubles as a floatation device.

Believe in magic.

Remember that life
is a great adventure.